FRIENDS
OF ACPL

3 1833 04624 8883

D1064205

CELEBRITY BIOS

Tobey Maguire

Philip Abraham

HIGH
interest
books

Children's Press®
A Division of Scholastic Inc.
New York / Toronto / London / Auckland / Sydney
Mexico City / New Delhi / Hong Kong
Danbury, Connecticut

Book Design: Michael DeLisio
Contributing Editor: Scott Waldman

Photo Credits: Cover © Jeff Spicer/Alpha/Globe Photos, Inc.; pp. 4, 11, 14, 16, 18, 21, 23 © Everett Collection, Inc.; pp. 24, 26, 29, 30, 33, 34 © Columbia Pictures/ courtesy Everett Collection, Inc.; p. 8 © Bob Villard/Globe Photos, Inc.; p. 37 © Bruce Cotler/Globe Photos, Inc.; p. 38 © Steve Finn/Alpha/Globe Photos, Inc.

Library of Congress Cataloging-in-Publication Data

Abraham, Philip, 1970–
  Tobey Maguire / Philip Abraham.
    p. cm. — (Celebrity bios)
  Includes index.
  Summary: A biography of the actor who has achieved fame for his leading
    roles in such movies as "The Cider House Rules" and "Spider-Man."
  ISBN 0-516-24334-9 (lib. bdg.) — ISBN 0-516-27862-2 (pbk.)
  1. Maguire, Tobey, 1975—Juvenile literature. 2. Actors—United
States—Biography—Juvenile literature. [1. Maguire, Tobey, 1975–2.
Actors and actresses.] I. Title. II. Series.

PN2287.M24 A25 2003
791.43'028'092—dc21

                                                      2002153282

Copyright © 2003 by Rosen Book Works, Inc.
All rights reserved. Published simultaneously in Canada.
Printed in the United States of America.
1 2 3 4 5 6 7 8 9 10 R 12 11 10 09 08 07 06 05 04 03

CONTENTS

CHAPTER ONE

Traveling Lad

"I look back and feel it must have been tough on my parents. Because of the times, I would be embarrassed by rolling up in the four-hundred-dollar, beat-up orange truck, or getting groceries with food stamps."

—Tobey, talking to *CNN.com* about his childhood

Tobey Maguire is currently one of the most sought-after actors of his generation. He has proven that he can play complex roles in serious movies, such as *The Cider House Rules*. He has also proven himself as an action hero. Tobey played the lead role in the Hollywood

From a childhood filled with many uncertainties, Tobey rose to become one of Hollywood's hottest stars.

blockbuster movie *Spider-Man*. He is known for playing sensitive, smart, yet troubled young men. Tobey's talent has made him one of today's hottest stars.

So how did Tobey wind up at the top of Hollywood's A-list of celebrities? To find out, we have to start with Tobey's earliest years.

ALWAYS ON THE MOVE

Tobias Vincent Maguire was born in Santa Monica, California, on June 27, 1975. Tobey's childhood was filled with a lot of uncertainty. His parents, Vincent and Wendy, were very young when they had Tobey. His mother was eighteen. His father was twenty. Tobey's dad worked as a construction worker and as a cook. His mother did secretarial work. Tobey's parents got divorced when he was very young.

After his parents were divorced, Tobey moved back and forth between his mother and father. He spent his early years in the Pacific

Northwest, growing up in California, Oregon, and Washington. "My mother and father weren't together for very long," he told *TeenHollywood.com.* "They would bounce around, and I would live in different situations."

All this moving around made it hard for Tobey to make friends. Tobey explained to *GQ* magazine: "When I was a teenager, I felt like I wouldn't give myself to anybody—meaning friends or relationships. I needed to be able to walk away at any point, which I think has served me well in some ways and then not so well in others."

Despite the challenges, Tobey has no regrets about his childhood. He does not have bad feelings about his experiences either. He told *USA Weekend,* "I wouldn't change anything about my life because it made me who I am. But some stability would've been nice. It's rough when you just begin to make friends, and then you've got to move again and again."

PAID TO ACT

Tobey's father was a good cook. Tobey gets his love of cooking from him. In fact, as a child, Tobey planned to become a chef. However, Wendy had other plans for her son. She had always wanted to be an actress but was unable to follow her dream. She urged Tobey to try acting. He was hesitant. Tobey wanted to study cooking in school. His mom came up with a plan to get him to try acting. She paid him a hundred dollars to take acting lessons.

Tobey discovered that he was very good at acting. Acting also made him more relaxed in school. In the eighth grade, he decided to go to a professional acting school. His ninth-grade teacher, Jimmy Lennon Jr., told *GQ,* "Tobey was a little more natural, a little more verbal than other kids. He wasn't with the in-crowd, but he was very well liked."

In 1989, Tobey earned his Screen Actors Guild card when he appeared in a Rodney Dangerfield TV comedy special. The card meant that Tobey was now a member of an actor's union. For the TV special, Tobey was given a hotel room in Las Vegas and received $80 a day for his expenses. This proved to be a pretty exciting experience for a fourteen-year-old boy.

Moving around to so many different places was taking a toll on Tobey. He frequently missed school and got into many arguments with his mother. Nevertheless, Tobey was

Tobey and Leonardo DiCaprio have been friends since they were teens. However, they refuse to talk about each other's performances in movies.

becoming more and more interested in acting. Sometime around tenth grade acting became his biggest passion.

In 1990, Tobey dropped out of high school to concentrate on his acting career full time. He eventually earned his high school equivalency through home study. Soon, Tobey was going on many auditions. During this time, Tobey lived with his mother in Hollywood. Being a good actor was very important to Tobey. He studied books about acting. Al Pacino and Robert De Niro were two of his favorite actors. Tobey studied their movies.

Tobey landed small parts in several TV shows, such as *Blossom* and *Roseanne*. Then, in 1992, he won the lead role in a sitcom on the Fox network. *Great Scott!* starred Tobey as Scott Melrod, a teenager with an active imagination. Unfortunately, the show did not catch on with TV audiences. It was canceled after just nine weeks.

In his television show, *Great Scott!* Tobey played a teenager whose wacky imagination got him into trouble.

Tobey didn't allow himself to become discouraged by the failure of *Great Scott!* He continued to audition for other TV shows as well as movies. In 1993, he tried out for the lead role in the movie *This Boy's Life*. The movie was set in the Pacific Northwest in the 1950s.

The story was about the travels of a boy and his mother and their search for a better life. Obviously, Tobey could identify with the main character's desire for a stable childhood. Ellen Barkin played the mother. Robert De Niro played the mother's boyfriend who clashes with the boy. About four hundred other hopeful young actors auditioned. Leonardo DiCaprio, longtime friend of Tobey's, got the part. During his audition, Tobey got very nervous doing a screen test with De Niro. However, Tobey still got a small role in the movie.

ACTING SUCCESS

Tobey continued to get roles in television and movies. In 1995, Tobey made the decision to stop going out a lot at night. Instead of spending too much time socializing, he stayed home and read scripts. He had decided to devote the rest of his life to acting.

Tobey's big break came when he was cast in the short film *Duke of Groove*. The director, Griffin Dunne, cast Tobey as the film's lead, Rich Cooper. Cooper is a teenager who accompanies his mother to a party. As the night unfolds, he learns that she and his father are getting divorced. To prepare for the role, Dunne had Tobey read J.D. Salinger's *The Catcher in the Rye* and watch *The Graduate*. The main characters of the book and the movie were young men struggling to find their place in the world. *Duke of Groove* was nominated for an Oscar for Best Short Film.

Did You Know?

Tobey had a small role in the 1995 movie *Empire Records.* However, all of the scenes in which he appeared, were cut out when the movie was released.

CHAPTER TWO

An Outsider's Path to Success

"I'm not sure why I play outsiders."

—Tobey, in an interview with *E! Online*

Tobey's acting in *Duke of Groove* brought him to the attention of the producers of *The Ice Storm*. In this 1997 movie, Tobey played Paul Hood. Paul quietly watches his family argue during Thanksgiving break. He is caught in the middle of all their problems. Once again, Tobey had found a story that reflected his own experiences. He told *Interview,* "It was also about something I could relate to. I wasn't living

Pleasantville was one of Tobey's first starring roles. The movie was shot in both black-and-white and color.

it at that moment, but it was close enough that I could still feel it and at the same time bring some humor to it." When director Ang Lee and the film's screenwriter, James Schamus, saw Tobey's audition tape, they agreed that he was perfect for the part.

Tobey's success began to grow. He continued to look for roles that would chal-

Working with the legendary director Woody Allen on *Deconstructing Harry* was a big thrill for young Tobey.

lenge him as an actor and as a person. Also in 1997, Tobey had a small role in Woody Allen's *Deconstructing Harry*. He played Harvey Stern. Stern was an imaginary character thought up by Woody Allen's character.

HAVING A PLEASANT TIME

In 1998, Tobey starred in *Pleasantville*. In this movie, Tobey played David. David was a teenager who spent most of his free time watching a 1950s black-and-white sitcom called *Pleasantville*. Thanks to a magical television remote control, David and his sister are transported into the fictional TV world of *Pleasantville*. Tobey's sister was played by Reese Witherspoon. Again, Tobey played a character who was seen as an outsider and was awkward around people. The movie was written and directed by Gary Ross who wrote the Tom Hanks comedy *Big*.

OLD FRIENDS AND NEW CHALLENGES

In 1999, Tobey teamed up again with director Ang Lee and screenwriter James Schamus to make *Ride With the Devil*. The movie is set in the West at the beginning of the American Civil War. Tobey played Jake Roedel, a Southern

In *Ride With the Devil,* Tobey proved that he was capable of playing a wide variety of roles.

soldier. Roedel is out for revenge against a handful of Northern soldiers who had burned down a farm and killed the owners. The owners of the farm were friends of Roedel. Tobey costarred with Skeet Ulrich and singer-actress Jewel. Tobey was Ang Lee's first choice for the role of Jake Roedel. Lee saw how Tobey had changed as a person and as an actor since they had last worked together. He told *Premiere* magazine, "I had the pleasure to start [with Tobey] when he was really innocent, in

The Ice Storm, and then to see him grow from that innocence and pick up skills and be able to carry a whole, heavy-duty movie. As a person and as an actor, the innocence is no longer the only thing he has."

THE RULES OF SUCCESS

Ride With the Devil was not as successful as Tobey and the filmmakers hoped it would be. However, Tobey's luck was about to change in a big way. His second movie that was released in 1999 was *The Cider House Rules*. This movie was adapted from the acclaimed novel by well-known writer John Irving. Tobey starred with Charlize Theron, Michael Caine, Erykah Badu, and Delroy Lindo. Tobey played Homer Wells. Homer was an orphan who was adopted and raised by his orphanage's doctor, Wilbur Larch.

Did You Know?

To prepare for his role as a Civil War soldier in *Ride With the Devil*, Tobey did not wash or shower for several weeks.

19

Larch, played by Michael Caine, trains Homer to become a doctor. The movie is about Homer struggling to come to terms with his destiny. Does he stay at the orphanage and carry on the work that Dr. Larch has trained him for? Or does he go off into the world by himself? The movie was a hit with both moviegoers and movie critics. It won two Academy Awards. Michael Caine won the Best Supporting Actor award. John Irving won an award for his screenplay.

A WONDERFUL ROLE

Tobey was on a roll, landing good parts in critically acclaimed movies. In 2000, he starred with Michael Douglas in *The Wonder Boys*. Tobey played the character of James Leer. Leer is a troubled college student and writer. Leer has a stormy father-son type relationship with his writing professor. Michael Douglas plays the professor. Tobey told *E! Online,*

Tobey got to be good friends with Michael Douglas during the filming of *The Wonder Boys*.

"On [*The*] *Wonder Boys*, it was wonderful going to work with Michael Douglas every day because he's so engaging. We both like basketball a lot, so I would come to his trailer and watch some games, and we would chat about basketball."

Movie critics began to take notice of the young actor. Many of them thought he was taking a minimalist approach to his acting style. Minimalist style means the actor holds back emotions or actions in his or her character's portrayal. Critics wondered if Tobey was like that in real life. Tobey described his acting to *E! Online*: "In *The Cider House Rules*, I was holding back very much on purpose. I wanted Homer Wells to be a very restrained person—and James in [*The*] *Wonder Boys* is very similar in that way. Both of them reveal only so much of themselves to other people. It's not me, Tobey, being that way—it's the choices I made for the characters."

LETTING THE FUR FLY

In his next movie, Tobey went in a completely different direction. Tobey was *heard* but not seen in the 2001 comedy *Cats and Dogs*. Tobey is the voice of the movie's hero, Lou the Beagle. The movie is about a secret war waged between cats and dogs for world domination. Computer effects and lifelike puppets were used to make the animals look like they were doing amazing things, such as cats fighting like

Tobey's character in *Cats and Dogs*, Lou the Beagle, battles against his foe's plan of world domination. His rival is Mr. Tinkles, an evil cat.

ninjas. The movie did well at the box office. Tobey's biggest box office hit, however, was about to come.

CHAPTER THREE

Does Whatever a Spider Can

"I'm not worried about being pegged as only Spider-Man or a superhero. I waited long enough in my career to show that I obviously have other characters in me."

—Tobey, in *People* magazine

In 2000, Tobey shocked the Hollywood community when he landed the role of Spider-Man. Spider-Man has been the star of his own line of comic books since the early 1960s. Most people thought the role would go to an actor who was known as an action star.

Before *Spider-Man*, Tobey was a successful actor. Since the movie's incredible success, his career has spun out of control!

In this photo, director Sam Raimi is explaining a scene from *Spider-Man* to Tobey and Kirsten Dunst.

Many people thought a Spider-Man movie would be heavy on action, at the expense of good storytelling and acting. However, Sam Raimi, the movie's director, knew better. He wanted Spider-Man and his alter ego, Peter Parker, to seem real to audiences. Raimi told *USA Weekend,* "When the camera gets close on Peter, the audience will know whether he has a good soul. You can't fake it. Tobey is soulful. He's aware of a lot of life within and around him, more than other men his age. This is a complex, character-driven picture, and

Tobey's the only guy who could've made it work."

Though Sam Raimi wanted Tobey to star in *Spider-Man,* the movie studio executives at Columbia Pictures did not want Tobey. The studio was going to spend millions of dollars making the movie. They wanted a big-name star to play Spider-Man. Among the actors considered for the role were Heath Ledger, Chris O'Donnell, Wes Bentley, and Chris Klein. Tobey had to audition two times before studio executives were convinced that he would make a good Spider-Man.

Tobey's first screen test was a romantic scene between Peter Parker and Mary Jane. The second screen test was an action scene. For this test, Tobey dressed in a unitard, or skin-tight suit, similar to the Spider-Man costume. Tobey explained to *Wizard,* a magazine about comic books, "I wore a unitard thing—like a full blue suit. I did an entire fight scene for them [the

27

studio executives]. By the middle of the scene, I had shed the top layer and tied it off at my waist. So I went topless and finished this kind of martial arts fight scene. It was a good-looking screen test, and I think it finally clicked with them that I could play both [Peter Parker and Spider-Man]."

Raimi told *Entertainment Weekly,* "The strength of Spider-Man is that Peter is a character we identify with as a normal middle-class kid. We needed someone who was completely vulnerable and lived with a certain amount of doubt and angst. And Tobey was so grounded and subtle, I simply believed him."

Spider-Man producer Laura Ziskin was also taken with Tobey's personality. She told *Time*

Did You Know?

Before landing the role of Spider-Man, Tobey had never read a Spider-Man comic book or seen any of the TV shows.

The role of Spider-Man had Tobey acting in ways he had never done before!

magazine, "Tobey's an everyman. He's adorable, but he's not the classic hunk. He's not a model. He looks like an ordinary kid."

Tobey could identify with the problems Spider-Man faced. He summed these up for *USA Weekend:* "Here's a very normal young man, Peter Parker, who goes from being unpopular, intelligent, and awkward around girls to a superhero. The responsibility, the loneliness, the sacrifices—I went through some of these themes in my life."

GETTING IN SHAPE

Tobey needed to be in good shape to wear the Spider-Man costume. He also had to be fit enough to do some of the physical action. To get ready for the role, he worked out a lot.

Tobey spent about four hours a day, six days a week, toning up. He also lifted weights to build muscles. He did aerobic exercises and yoga to make sure he could stretch and assume all of Spider-Man's poses. Tobey also performed martial arts and gymnastics to help burn

body fat. All of this intense training went on for about five months. Since Tobey is a vegetarian, he ate a special diet. Some of the things he ate included high-protein shakes, tofu, broccoli, walnuts, veggie burgers, and brown rice.

Tobey kept to a rigid exercise and diet program for six days out of the week. On the seventh day though, he relaxed. He told *E! Online*, ". . . I could eat whatever I wanted. One thing I love to do is go to a Laker game or a movie and just eat popcorn and M&Ms and stuff. So, I would always go see a movie or a game on a Sunday. I couldn't sustain something so strict without a little break here and there."

SWINGING INTO ACTION

Playing Spider-Man presented a unique challenge for Tobey. Since Spider-Man wears a mask, the audience can't see Tobey's face. Tobey had to work on showing what Spider-Man was feeling through his body language.

Even though Tobey spent a lot of time in the weight room for his role as Spider-Man, his on-screen muscles were computer enhanced.

Tobey communicated the feelings of his character through gestures, movements, and mannerisms. It worked like a charm. Audiences loved Tobey's portrayal of the superhero.

HANGING OUT

One of the most talked-about scenes in *Spider-Man* was the scene where Spider-Man hangs upside down in the rain. Physically, it was a hard scene for Tobey to shoot. The weight training he had done in preparation for the movie certainly helped. Tobey had to hang off a fire escape while the scene was being shot. Tobey explained the experience to *E! Online:* "It was tough. I was hanging upside down, it was five in the morning, I'd been working all night, it was raining, and water was pouring up my nose. I couldn't breathe through the mask, so I was sucking in and could barely get any air."

All of Tobey's hard work paid off. Moviegoers loved *Spider-Man*. The movie

While in costume as Spider-Man, Tobey had to learn how to express emotions, such as fear and anger, through body language.

made a record-breaking $114 million in its opening weekend. The movie would go on to earn just over $400 million by the end of its theatrical run in the United States alone!

CHAPTER FOUR

An Amazing Future

"I just want to make good movies. If there's a script I like with a character I like and a filmmaker I like, I would do the movie. I'm not really concerned about money."

—Tobey, in *Time* magazine

The stunning success of *Spider-Man* has changed Tobey's life forever. He is now one of the most recognizable Hollywood celebrities. Everyone wants to meet him and know about him. Tobey told *Time,* "It's kind of [strange]

Though Tobey was the first to play Spider-Man in a movie, the web-crawling character was created in the 1963 comic book by Stan Lee.

because it's pretty drastic. It's a more definitive difference than I expected. I feel like a lot of things changed within a three-day period."

Despite his star status, Tobey remains very private about his personal life. He refuses to discuss whom he is dating or has dated. Rumors circulated that Tobey and his on-screen love interest in *Spider-Man,* Kirsten Dunst, had become an item offscreen. Both denied the rumors.

PLAYING HARD

Tobey not only works very hard, he plays hard as well. Tobey loves basketball. He also enjoys playing backgammon and poker. He does both with a lot of drive and determination. Tobey relaxes with a close group of friends. One of them, director Morgan J. Freeman, explained to *USA Weekend* what it's like to play poker and backgammon with Tobey. Freeman said,

Tobey also stays involved in politics. In this photo, he is attending a political convention in Los Angeles.

"He's intent on annihilating anybody at the table. It gets even worse with backgammon, the game of choice. We've had twelve-hour sessions of pure mental warfare."

CHARGING INTO THE FUTURE

Tobey is determined to continue to push his career in new directions and take on new challenges. He is interested in producing movies.

An Amazing Future

He is one of the producers of Spike Lee's *The 25th Hour,* which is a movie about a man's last day before going to jail. Also, he has signed on to produce and star in *Seabiscuit.* In this movie, Tobey will play a 1930s jockey. The movie is based on a real-life story about a famous racehorse, Seabiscuit, and Red Pollard, the jockey who rode him. The movie will re-team Tobey with his *Pleasantville* director, Gary Ross. About having Tobey in the role of Red Pollard, Gary Ross told *Variety,* "There was an incredible toughness and sensitivity to Red that few people could capture, and Tobey is uniquely capable of doing that." For his work on the movie, Tobey will receive $12 million!

After filming is complete on *Seabiscuit,* Tobey will once again put on his Spider-Man costume to film the sequel to the hit 2002 movie. For Tobey, the future holds a web of possibilities and all of them are amazing!

After playing a jockey and revisiting his Spider-Man character, who knows what role Tobey will take on next!

TIMELINE

1975   • Tobey is born on June 27 in Santa Monica, California.

1989   • Tobey gets his first professional acting role in *On Location: Rodney Dangerfield Opening Night at Rodney's Place.*

1990   • Tobey leaves school to concentrate on acting.

1991   • Tobey appears in the TV shows *Blossom* and *Eerie, Indiana*.

1992   • Tobey lands the lead role in the TV comedy *Great Scott!*

1993   • Tobey appears on the TV drama *Walker, Texas Ranger*. He gets a small role in the movie *This Boy's Life*.

1994   • Tobey appears in the TV movies *A Child's Cry for Help* and *Spoils of War*. He also appears in the movie *S.F.W.*

1995   • Tobey gets the lead role in the short film *Duke of Groove*. Also, he has a small role in *Empire Records*.

1996   • Tobey appears in the TV movie *Seduced by Madness: The Diane Borchardt Story* and the film *Joyride*.

TIMELINE

1997
- Tobey has his first important role in a major Hollywood movie playing Paul Hood in Ang Lee's *The Ice Storm*. He gets a small role in the Woody Allen movie *Deconstructing Harry*.

1998
- Tobey has a role in the movie *Fear and Loathing in Las Vegas*. He stars with Reese Witherspoon in the movie *Pleasantville*.

1999
- Tobey once again works with Ang Lee to make the Civil War movie *Ride With the Devil*. Tobey stars in the highly acclaimed movie *The Cider House Rules*.

2000
- Tobey stars with Michael Douglas in *The Wonder Boys*. Tobey is cast as Spider-Man.

2001
- Tobey lends his voice to Lou the Beagle, the hero of the family comedy *Cats and Dogs*.

2002
- Tobey stars as Spider-Man in *Spider-Man*. Tobey coproduces the movie *The 25th Hour*. Also, he agrees to coproduce and star in *Seabiscuit: An American Legend*.

2004
- Tobey stars in the second Spider-Man movie.

FACT SHEET

Name	Tobias Vincent Maguire
Born	June 27, 1975
Birthplace	Santa Monica, California
Family	Father: Vincent; Mother: Wendy; Half brothers: Vincent and Timothy; Half sister: Sara
Height	5'8"
Hair	Brown
Eyes	Blue
Sign	Cancer

Favorites

Actor	Robert De Niro
Food	Vegetarian
Sport	Basketball
Hobbies	Backgammon, yoga

NEW WORDS

adapted (uh-**dapt**-tuhd) to have adjusted a story, play, or novel for presentation as a television show or movie

audition (aw-**dish**-uhn) a short performance by an actor, singer, musician, or dancer to see whether he or she is suitable for a part in a movie, a play, a concert, etc.

cynical (**sin**-uh-kuhl) always expecting the worst to happen and thinking that anything people do is for selfish reasons

destiny (**dess**-tuh-nee) a course of events in your life that is unavoidable

domination (**dom**-uh-nay-shuhn) rule over another

minimalist (**min**-uh-muhl-ist) a person whose style or technique is characterized by extreme spareness and simplicity

role (**rohl**) the part that a person acts in a movie, a television show, a play, etc.

union (**yoon**-yuhn) an organized group of workers set up to help improve such things as working conditions, wages, and health benefits

vegetarian (vej-uh-**ter**-ee-uhn) someone who eats only plants and plant products and sometimes eggs or dairy products

vulnerable (**vulh**-nur-uh-buhl) likely to be hurt or damaged in some way

FOR FURTHER READING

Books

David, Peter. *Spider-Man*. New York: Del Rey Books, 2002.

Stevens, Chambers. *Sensational Scenes for Teens*. South Pasadena, California: Sandcastle Publishing, 2001.

Vaz, Mark Cotta. *Behind the Mask of Spider-Man: The Secrets of the Movie*. New York: Del Rey Books, 2002.

FOR FURTHER READING

Magazines

Cinescape
12456 Ventura Boulevard, Suite 2
Studio City, CA 91604
www.cinescape.com

Entertainment Weekly
1675 Broadway, 29th floor
New York, NY 10019
www.ew.com

People
Time & Life Building
Rockefeller Center
New York, NY 10020-1393
www.people.com

RESOURCES

Web Sites

Tobey Maguire Online
http://tobeyonline.com/index2.html
This is an unofficial Web site dedicated to the life
and career of Tobey Maguire. The site offers a brief
biography, interviews, articles, and the latest news
on Tobey's career. The site also has a photo gallery
and games.

Internet Movie Database—Toby Maguire
http://us.imdb.com/Name?Maguire,+Tobey
Check out Tobey's Internet Movie Database page.
You can find information on all of his movie and
TV roles.

You can write to Tobey at:

Tobey Maguire
c/o The Gersh Agency
P.O. Box 5617
Beverly Hills, CA 90120

INDEX

INDEX

About the Author

Philip Abraham is a freelance writer. He has written many books for children and young adults.